Benjamin Zephaniah   ILLUSTRATED BY Onyinye Iwu

We Sang Across the Sea
The Empire Windrush and Me

EMPIRE   WINDRU

FOR AGES 5–7

Published in the UK by Scholastic, 2023

Scholastic Distribution Centre, Bosworth Avenue, Tournament Fields, Warwick, CV34 6UQ

Scholastic Ireland, 89E Lagan Road, Dublin Industrial Estate, Glasnevin, Dublin, D11 HP5F

SCHOLASTIC and associated logos are trademarks and/or registered trademarks of Scholastic Inc.

© 2023 Scholastic Limited

www.scholastic.co.uk

1 2 3 4 5 6 7 8 9   3 4 5 6 7 8 9 0 1 2

A CIP catalogue record for this book is available from the British Library.
ISBN 978-0702-31957-0

Printed and bound by Ashford Colour Press
The book is made of materials from well-managed,
FSC®-certified forests and other controlled sources.

Extracts from *The National Curriculum in England, English Programme of Study* © Crown Copyright. Reproduced under the terms of the Open Government Licence (OGL). http://www.nationalarchives.gov.uk/doc/open-government-licence/version/3

Author Samantha Pope

Editorial team Rachel Morgan, Vicki Yates, Jo Kemp, Liz Evans

Series designer Andrea Lewis

Typesetter QBS Learning

Illustrator Giovana Medeiros

Photographs page 14: armadillo, Christopher Biggs/Shutterstock; page 29: Mona Baptiste, United Archives GmbH/Alamy Stock Photo

Acknowledgements

The publishers gratefully acknowledge permission to reproduce the following copyright material: **Scholastic UK** for the use of the Extract and illustrations from *We Sang Across the Sea* by Benjamin Zephaniah, text copyright © 2022 Benjamin Zephaniah, illustrations copyright © Onyinye Iwu.

Every effort has been made to trace copyright holders for the works reproduced in this book, and the publishers apologise for any inadvertent omissions.

For supporting online resources go to:
www.scholastic.co.uk/read-and-respond/books/we-sang-across-the-sea/online-resources
Access key: Lastly

CONTENTS ▼

How to use Read & Respond in your classroom...

Read & Respond provides teaching ideas related to a specific well-loved children's book. Each Read & Respond book is divided into the following sections:

ABOUT THE BOOK AND AUTHOR

Gives you some background information about the book and the author.

GUIDED READING

Breaks the book down into sections and gives notes for using it, ideal for use with the whole class. A bookmark has been provided on page 10 containing **comprehension** questions. The children can be directed to refer to these as they read. Find comprehensive guided reading sessions on the supporting online resources.

SHARED READING

Provides extracts from the children's book with associated notes for focused work. There is also one non-fiction extract that relates to the children's book.

PHONICS & SPELLING

Provides word-level work related to the children's book so you can teach phonics, spelling and **vocabulary** in context.

PLOT, CHARACTER & SETTING

Contains activity ideas focused on the plot, character and setting of the story.

TALK ABOUT IT

Oracy, **fluency**, and speaking and listening activities. These activities may be based directly on the children's book or be broadly based on the themes and concepts of the story.

GET WRITING

Provides writing activities related to the children's book. These activities may be based directly on the children's book or be broadly based on the themes and concepts of the story.

ASSESSMENT

Contains short activities that will help you assess whether the children have understood concepts and curriculum objectives. They are designed to be informal activities to feed into your planning.

SUPPORTING ONLINE RESOURCE

Online you can find a host of supporting documents including planning information, comprehensive guided reading sessions and guidance on teaching reading.

www.scholastic.co.uk/read-and-respond/books/
we-sang-across-the-sea/online-resources
Access key: Lastly

Help children develop a love of reading for pleasure.

Activities

The activities follow the same format:

- **Objective:** the objective for the lesson. It will be based upon a curriculum objective, but will often be more specific to the focus being covered.

- **What you need:** a list of resources you need to teach the lesson, including photocopiable pages.

- **What to do:** the activity notes.

- **Differentiation:** this is provided where specific and useful differentiation advice can be given to support and/or extend the learning in the activity. Differentiation by providing additional adult support has not been included as this will be at a teacher's discretion based upon specific children's needs and ability, as well as the availability of support.

The activities are numbered for reference within each section and should move through the text sequentially – so you can use the lesson while you are reading the book. Once you have read the book, most of the activities can be used in any order you wish.

Section	Activity	Curriculum objectives
Guided reading		Comprehension: To participate in discussion about what is read to them, taking turns and listening to what others say; to explain clearly their understanding of what is read to them.
Shared reading	1	Comprehension: To draw on what they already know or on background information and vocabulary provided by the teacher.
	2	Comprehension: To discuss and clarify the meaning of words, linking new meaning to known vocabulary.
	3	Comprehension: To listen to and discuss a wide range of poems, stories and non-fiction.
Phonics & spelling	1	Transcription: To use the spelling rule for adding 's' or 'es' as the plural marker for nouns.
	2	Transcription: To know that adding the ending 'ing' to verbs where no change is needed to the root word adds an extra syllable to the word.
	3	Spoken language: To use relevant strategies to build their vocabulary.
	4	Transcription: To use 'ed' where no change is needed in the spelling of root words.
Plot, character & setting	1	Comprehension: To discuss and clarify the meaning of words, linking new meanings to known vocabulary.
	2	Comprehension: To discuss the significance of events.
	3	Composition: To read aloud their writing clearly enough to be heard by their peers and the teacher.
	4	Spoken language: To give well-structured descriptions, explanations and narratives for different purposes, including for expressing feelings.
	5	Comprehension: To participate in discussion about what is read to them, taking turns and listening to what others say.
	6	Spoken language: To ask relevant questions to extend their understanding and knowledge.
Talk about it	1	Spoken language: To listen and respond appropriately to adults and their peers.
	2	Comprehension: To make inferences on the basis of what is being said and done.
	3	Spoken language: To participate in discussions, presentations, performances, role play, improvisations and debates.
	4	Spoken language: To consider and evaluate different viewpoints, attending to and building on the contributions of others.
	5	Comprehension: To link what they read or hear to their own experiences.
	6	Spoken language: To articulate and justify answers, arguments and opinions.
Get writing	1	Composition: To say out loud what they are going to write about.
	2	Vocabulary, grammar and punctuation: To begin to punctuate sentences using a capital letter and a full stop, question mark or exclamation mark.
	3	Composition: To sequence sentences to form short narratives.
	4	Composition: To write narratives about personal experiences and those of others.
	5	Composition: To discuss what they have written with the teacher or other pupils.
	6	Composition: To encapsulate what they want to say, sentence by sentence.
Assessment	1	Comprehension: To explain clearly their understanding of what is read to them.
	2	Vocabulary, grammar and punctuation: To learn how to use expanded noun phrases to describe and specify.
	3	Vocabulary, grammar and punctuation: To develop their understanding of the concepts set out in English Appendix 2 by joining words and joining clauses using 'and'.
	4	Spoken language: To use spoken language to develop understanding through speculating, hypothesising, imagining and exploring ideas.

Key facts

◉ **Title:**
We Sang Across the Sea

◉ **Author:**
Benjamin Zephaniah

◉ **Illustrator:**
Onyinye Iwu

◉ **First published:**
2022 by Scholastic Children's Books

◉ **Awards:**
Costa Biography Award shortlist (2018), Manchester Book Award (2006), British Book Awards Decibel Writer of the Year (2005), Portsmouth Book Award (2002), Commission for Racial Equality Race in the Media Radio Drama Award (2001), BBC Young Playwrights Festival Award (1988)

◉ **Did you know?**
Benjamin Zephaniah writes what is called 'dub poetry', which is a type of performance poetry that is sometimes set to music, particularly reggae. His works are mainly politically motivated.

About the book

Young Mona Baptiste just wants to do one thing in life: sing. She sings when she plays with her four sisters in Trinidad, she sings at carnivals and shows, and then she decides to try taking her singing to a wider audience when she sees an advertisement to travel to, and live in, England. It means leaving her home and family behind, but her dreams were urging her to follow this adventure of a lifetime. She travels on board the famous ship HMT *Empire Windrush* with other emigrants, many of whom are musicians too. There are some surprises in store for her when she arrives at her destination – not least the much cooler weather! However, Mona dedicates herself to her musical career and, despite some difficult times, becomes a 'singing sensation' not just in England but in much of the rest of Europe, including Germany, France and Ireland.

About the author

Dr Benjamin Zephaniah is a multi-award-winning poet, actor and musician. He was born in 1958 and raised in Handsworth, Birmingham and he cannot remember a time when he wasn't writing poetry. He left school aged only 13, unable to read or write because of dyslexia, but by the age of 15 he had a strong, local reputation as a poet who tackled important local, national and international issues. He says that his poetry is strongly influenced by Jamaican music and poetry and, after moving to London at the age of 22, he published his first volume called *Pen Rhythm*. From then on, his fame blossomed. Benjamin has also excelled in music and other forms of writing, including playwriting and novels. He has published two poetry collections for children: *Talking Turkeys* (1994) and *Funky Chickens* (1996). He has received numerous honorary doctorates, been named one of the top 50 post-war writers in *The Times*, and has won and been shortlisted for numerous awards, including the Costa Biography Award in 2018.

About the illustrator

Onyinye Iwu was born in Italy to Nigerian parents. She moved to the UK when she was a teenager and did a degree in Architecture, before following this with a PGCE in Design Technology and then a Master's degree in Culture Diaspora Ethnicity. She worked as a freelance illustrator and designer from 2013, but also undertook a career as a secondary school teacher in 2014, hoping to be a role model for other young black people. Most of her design work focuses on representing people of African and Caribbean backgrounds in publishing, media and the arts.

GUIDED READING ▶

Front and back covers

Together as a class, look at the front and back covers of the book before you start reading the story. Ask the children question 1 on the bookmark. Children might comment on the illustrations of people singing and dancing, the reference in the blurb on the back to 'the real-life story of Trinidadian musician, Mona Baptiste.' The repeated refrain is also on the back cover.

Getting the most from the book

As you read through the book together, pay special attention to expression, changing your tone of voice to suit the material. The story is written like a song, so have fun reading it and enjoy the rhythm and rhyme. Involve the children in the repeated refrains/choruses: 'I just want to sing…So, I just want to sing' – they will love joining in with you. Ensure that you stop regularly to check that they understand the meaning of words.

Discuss the use of punctuation. Zephaniah often uses commas at the end of lines, which is common in poetry. You can tell the children that commas are frequently used in poetry and that they help the reader pause briefly after every line.

Spreads 1 and 2

As you read through these first two spreads, explain that their purpose is to establish the scene, setting, characters and what the book is about.

Look closely at spreads 1 and 2, and ask question 3 on the bookmark. Many of the words relate to the weather: sunshine, pleasant breezes, eating fruit from the garden and playing on the beach, and the pictures show a family having fun in the sun. Ask: *Do you think that this is a good place to live?*

On spread 2, 'I want to be a singer' and 'Joy is what I bring, So, I just want to sing' are in larger letters than the rest of the text. Ask the children why. (Perhaps to emphasise, from the start, that Mona knows exactly what she wants to do when she is older.)

Ask the children question 2 on the bookmark. Ask: *Do they think she means that she will get taller? How else can a person grow? How does singing help with that?*

Spreads 3 and 4

Look at spread 3, which shows a typical Carnival scene. Use question 6 from the bookmark to discuss what the other people are doing at the Carnival while Mona sings. (Dancing and playing musical instruments.) Ask the children to describe the Carnival costumes. *How are they different from what Mona and the other adults around her are wearing?*

Move on to spread 4 and point out that Mona is not a girl any more in the picture on the left page. (She would have been 20 when she sailed.) Talk through the poster and point out the two ticket types for the *Empire Windrush*. Do the children think this is cheap? (It wouldn't have been then!) Ask: *Have you ever been on a boat? What was it like? Did you sleep on it?*

Read out the following line: 'If I could sing in England it would be a dream come true,' and ask: *Why was Mona so keen to become a singer in England, rather than in her own country?* (The music scene in the UK was much bigger then, with lots of opportunities.)

Spreads 5 and 6

Spread 5 focuses on the departure of the *Empire Windrush*. Ask the children to look at the facial expressions of the people on the boat. *How do they look?* (excited, happy, joyful) Can the children pick out Mona? (She's the one with the biggest smile.) Ask: *How does this compare with the statement, 'I was a little nervous, and a bit lonely, and a tear fell from my eye.' Why does Mona feel this way when she is on a very busy boat, about to make her dream come true?*

Next, ask the children what they think about question 8 on the bookmark. Say: *The illustration shows Mona's family waving cheerfully at Mona, but are they really happy?*

Look at spread 6 together and then ask the children to think about the answer to question 7 on the bookmark. (The repetition of the word 'many' emphasises the number of people on board the *Empire Windrush* – there were more than 1000 people.) This also shows the variety of people travelling to England, from different places and backgrounds. Ask: *How do you think Mona felt being among so many other musicians?* (Answers may vary: perhaps very happy to find others like herself, and less lonely.)

Spreads 7 and 8

Spread 7 shows Mona once she has arrived in England, and spread 8 shows her in France with friends. Ask the children question 4 on the bookmark. Interestingly, it looks sunny, despite the words: 'When I arrived in England it was cool.' Ask: *How can you tell that they are in Paris on spread 8?* (The Eiffel Tower is in the background!)

Draw children's attention to what the people are wearing. Ask: *How are the clothes different from what people wear nowadays?* (To the children, they will appear more formal – men often wore ties, women wore mainly dresses and skirts and many more people wore hats.)

On spread 7, Mona talks about 'singing everywhere, so people would get to know my name' – explain that this is what the word 'recognition' in the next line means. Ask the children why the little girl sitting in front of the television looks so surprised. (Answers could include that not many black women were on television then.) Draw their attention to the size of the TV compared with the TVs nowadays.

Spreads 9 and 10

On spread 9, we see a different side to Mona's previously cheerful character. Ask the children why this could be, using question 9 on the bookmark. (She may be nervous – mention the term 'stage fright' and what it means. Have any of the children ever felt that way before?). Look at the words 'As a Caribbean girl, sometimes I just had to be quite strong.' Ask: *What does she mean by this and why does she especially think it's because she's Caribbean?* (In Europe, black people were in a minority then and not everyone was happy to welcome them.)

Mona also admits that 'Sometimes I needed someone to help me turn the page.' *What does she mean by this?* (Sometimes she needed someone else to help her find her confidence and bravery. Ask the children if they have ever needed help in this way.) When she is on the stage on the right-hand page, can the children see any signs of the nervousness or fear? *Why is she different now?*

Spread 10 is the last one in the book. Ask the children who they think all the people gathered round Mona are (probably her family and friends). Then ask question 5 on the bookmark. (Answers could include that the author and illustrator wanted to show Mona with her family again.) You could mention that it gives a feeling of completeness, finishing as it started, with Mona and her family happy together. Point out the final 'chorus' of the book and how it is different from the others as it is in the past tense, for example, 'I wanted to sing'. Ask the children why the writer chose to do this (to show the reader that Mona followed her dream and that becoming a singer did help her grow).

What did the children think of the story? Use question 10 on the bookmark to gather opinions about the ending from the class.

At some point here, or in the activities, you could play some recordings of Mona Baptiste singing, which can be found on the internet.

We Sang Across the Sea

by Benjamin Zephaniah and Onyinye Iwu

Focus on...
Meaning

1. Why is the book called *We Sang Across the Sea*?

2. What does Mona mean when she says that 'Singing songs will help me grow'?

Focus on...
Organisation

3. From the first two spreads, what are the author and illustrator telling you about life in Trinidad?

4. How does life in England and France look compared with Mona's childhood in Trinidad?

5. Why does the book end in a house instead of on a stage, for example?

We Sang Across the Sea

by Benjamin Zephaniah and Onyinye Iwu

Focus on...
Language and features

6. Mona is singing at the Carnival on spread 3, but what are the other people doing?

7. On spread 6, Benjamin Zephaniah repeats the word 'many' four times. Why?

Focus on...
Purpose, viewpoints and effects

8. On spread 5, we don't see the expressions on Mona's family's faces. Why has the illustrator not shown them? How do you think they feel?

9. Why do you think Mona looks so scared to go on stage towards the end of the book?

10. Did the book end in a good way or would you have liked to know more about Mona?

SHARED READING ▶

Extract 1

- Display an enlarged copy of Extract 1. Read it aloud and ask the children: *How is Mona feeling?* Children should identify nervous, worried or sad. Ask: *Why is 'a tear fell from my eye' written in larger letters than the other words?* (They emphasise Mona's feelings as she leaves her family.)
- Next, circle the words: 'nervous', 'lonely' and 'tear' and ask the children if they know what they mean. Model how you would use them in sentences.
- Tell the children you are going to play a game called 'Three Times'. In this game, each child tries to think of three times when:
  - they were nervous
  - they have felt lonely
  - they cried.
- Model the answers yourself first, then ask the children to share their answers. Since this can be an emotive activity, ensure that you handle it sensitively and that the children are sensitive to each other's examples.

Extract 2

- Display an enlarged copy of Extract 2 and read through it with the class.
- Circle the word 'they' in the extract. Ask: *Who you think 'they' refers to?* (probably people in Europe who have heard Mona sing; perhaps people who have read about her in the newspaper, heard her on the radio or seen her on the television). Can the children suggest why Benjamin Zephaniah did not say who 'they' are? (Perhaps he felt these people were less important to the story, or maybe he wanted the reader to realise lots of different people were talking about Mona – too many to mention.)
- Next, circle the phrase 'I sang', which is repeated three times in the passage. Ask the children why this might be. (Perhaps it is to emphasise how many places Mona sang in.) Does it have any effect on the writing? (It creates rhythm.)
- Read aloud: 'But sometimes people still asked me, what did I want to do.' Ask: *As Mona is already a famous singer, why do people keep asking her what she wants to do?* (Perhaps because they don't think being a singer is a 'proper' job.)

Extract 3

- Tell the children that they are going to learn about Trinidad, the island where Mona Baptiste was born.
- Display a map of the Caribbean, with Trinidad and Tobago on it. Show how close it is to South America and how far away it is from the UK. Ask the children to predict what it might be like there, using any ideas they may have gained from *We Sang Across the Sea*.
- Next, read through Extract 3 with the children, explaining any new words.
- Ask: *What do you think life is like in Trinidad? Would you like to live there? Why or why not?*
- Next, ask them to tell you what some of the main similarities and differences are between living in Trinidad and in the UK (for example, similarities: they are both islands and English is the main language; differences: the animals and the food).
- Write the children's thoughts on the board.

Extract 1

My parents said, 'Good luck, Mona', and 'Take care',

As they waved,

My sisters looked at the great big ship, and they were
all amazed,

As the ship left the dock and we started to sail

They all waved goodbye,

I was a little nervous,

and a bit lonely, and a tear fell from my eye.

Extract 2

They called me the singing sensation,
   from far across the sea,
My family were proud, and so was I,
   when they talked about me.
I sang in Germany, I sang in France,
   I sang in Ireland too,
But sometimes people still asked me,
   what did I want to do.

Extract 3

Exploring Trinidad

Mona Baptiste was from a place called Trinidad, which is in the Caribbean Sea. Trinidad and another island called Tobago make up a country called The Republic of Trinidad and Tobago. The capital is Port of Spain. The main language is English.

Both Trinidad and Tobago have mountains and tropical rainforests. The weather is warm and dry but sometimes there is also lots of rain.

All sorts of interesting animals and birds can be found in Trinidad, such as golden tree frogs, porcupines, armadillos, leatherback turtles and the scarlet ibis – the country's national bird.

An armadillo

The best cocoa beans in the world are grown in Trinidad – and chocolate is made from them! The country is also famous for inventing the steelpan, which is its national instrument. The first ones were made from oil drums.

While Sunday lunch in the United Kingdom traditionally is a roast dinner, in Trinidad and Tobago it is 'crab and callaloo'. Callaloo sauce is a creamy mixture of green leaves, onions, okra pods, spicy peppers, butter, thyme and fresh coconut milk. You normally eat rice, dumplings or macaroni pie with it (yes – macaroni made into a creamy pie!).

PHONICS & SPELLING ▶

1. Making more than one

Objective
To use the spelling rule for adding 's' or 'es' as the plural marker for nouns.

What you need
Copies of *We Sang Across the Sea*, individual whiteboards.

What to do
- Ask the children if they know the rule for making noun endings plural. (If the ending of the word sounds like 's' or 'z', then you add an 's' at the end of the word. If the ending of the word sounds like 'iz', then add 'es'.) You might like to give a few examples of each to ensure the children understand the rule.

- Next, write on the board the following nouns from the book: 'sister', 'rain', 'parent', 'girl', 'island', 'morning', 'animal', 'thing'. Read each one aloud and ask the children how you should make them plural (add an 's' to the end).

- Finally, write the following words on the board (explaining that these are not from the book): 'fox', 'beach', 'push', 'itch', 'lunch', 'patch'. Say each word aloud and ask the children if they can tell you how to make them plural (add 'es' to the end). Can the children put the plural word into sentences? For example: *The foxes played in the moonlight.*

Differentiation
Extension: Challenge the children to look through the book to see further examples of plurals ending in 's' that they can make into singular nouns, for example: 'songs', 'lands', 'musicians', 'bands', 'skills', 'fruit'. Ask them to write these on their whiteboards.

2. Beat it!

Objective
To know that adding 'ing' to verbs where no change is needed to the root word adds an extra syllable.

What you need
Copies of *We Sang Across the Sea*.

What to do
- Ask the children if they know what a syllable is (part of a word that makes a sound or a 'beat').

- Explain that words have different numbers of syllables. Ask if anyone can give you an example of a word with one syllable. Take suggestions and then do the same for words of two and three syllables.

- Next, write the following words on the board:
  - Column 1: play, enjoy, dream, sing, sail
  - Column 2: playing, enjoying, dreaming, singing, sailing

- Read out the words in column 1 first, clapping as you do so. Can the children hear that the words only have one syllable, or beat? Do the same for the words in column 2, and ask: *Can you hear the extra syllable in these words?* Clap all the words together as a class.

- Explain to the children that adding 'ing' to verb endings where no change is needed to the root word adds an extra syllable to the word.

- Write the following infinitives from the book on the board: 'want', 'grow', 'know', 'start', 'ask', 'talk', 'bring'.

- Ask for volunteers to make these words two syllables, saying the word and clapping the syllables at the same time (wanting, growing, knowing, starting, asking, talking, bringing).

3. Have you ever?

> **Objective**
> To use relevant strategies to build their vocabulary.
>
> **What you need**
> Copies of *We Sang Across the Sea*.

What to do

- Write the words 'journey', 'musicians' and 'skills' on the board.

- Next, read spread 6 aloud to the children, where Mona meets the other travellers on the *Empire Windrush*. Instruct the children to listen out for the three words on the board.

- Return to the vocabulary and provide the children with a definition for each word, putting them into a sentence that is different from the one used in the story. For example:

  - The word 'journey' is used to describe when you travel from one place to another. You can have a journey from home to school or from England to another country, for example.
  - 'Musicians' are people who play music. For example, a piano player is a musician, and so is a singer or a drummer.
  - The word 'skills' means the things that a person is good at doing. For example, if you play football well, you have football skills.

- Once you feel confident that the children understand the meanings of the words, tell them you are going to play a game called 'Have You Ever…?' Write the following questions on the board:

  - Have you been on a journey anywhere? Tell us about it, using the word 'journey' in your answer.
  - Do you play any musical instruments, or sing? Tell me if you are a musician. Use the word 'musician' in your answer.
  - Do you have any skills? Tell me what you are good at and use the word 'skills' in your answer.

- You could model your answers to these questions to show the children how to do this before inviting them to answer.

4. From the present to the past

> **Objective**
> To use 'ed' where no change is needed in the spelling of root words.
>
> **What you need**
> Copies of *We Sang Across the Sea*, individual whiteboards.

What to do

- Tell the children that you are going to look at how to spell words in the past tense.

- First, ask if they know what a suffix is (an ending that you add to the root of a word).

- Next, ask if they can remember how to put a verb into the past tense. (You usually add 'ed' to the root word if it ends in two consonants or if the word ends in a vowel and a consonant.)

- As an example, write the following sentence from the book on the board: 'I started singing on the islands.' Underline the word 'started' and explain that 'start' is the present tense of the verb and 'started' is the past tense.

- Model a few examples orally, such as, 'thank' becomes 'thanked', 'chew' becomes 'chewed'.

- When you think the children are more confident with this rule, write a few verbs on the board, for example: 'touch', 'stay', 'trick'. Ask for volunteers to come up and change the root word into the past tense (for example, 'touch' becomes 'touched').

- Tell the children that you are going to write some verbs from *We Sang Across the Sea* on the board. Ask them to write each one on their whiteboards in the past tense, using the 'ed' suffix.

- Example words could include: 'want', 'sail', 'play', 'ask', 'work', 'call', 'talk', 'help'.

- When they have finished, ask the children to swap their whiteboards with someone else and mark the answers together.

> **Differentiation**
> **Extension:** Children write short sentences that include the words they have written.

PLOT, CHARACTER & SETTING ▶

1. Strange sayings

> **Objective**
> To discuss and clarify the meaning of words, linking new meanings to known vocabulary.
> **What to do**
> Copies of *We Sang Across the Sea.*

What to do

- Explain to the children that, while most of the words and phrases in the book are easy to understand, there are a few that might be trickier because they are expressions.

- Write the following expressions from the book on the board:

  - 'singing helped me to get along'
  - 'sometimes I had to be quite strong'
  - 'I needed someone to help me turn the page'
  - 'Singing really helped me grow'

- Ask the children if they know what each one means. Write down their answers/suggestions.

- Tell the children that sometimes we use expressions to add more interest to our writing or speaking but these are not meant to be taken literally. For example, do the children think that Mona had to be *physically* strong to cope with being a singer? Did someone else help her turn a page in a book or magazine?

- Explain what the sayings really mean:

  - 'singing helped me to get along' = singing helped Mona be more confident in herself
  - 'sometimes I had to be quite strong' = sometimes Mona had to overcome her fear to do what she needed to do
  - 'I needed someone to help me turn the page' = Mona needed someone to help her do what she needed to do
  - 'Singing really helped me grow' = singing helped Mona become a happier and more confident person.

2. From start to finish

> **Objective**
> To discuss the significance of events.
> **What you need**
> Copies of *We Sang Across the Sea*, individual whiteboards.

What to do

- Before the lesson, write the following on the board:

  1. Mona sang in Germany, France and Ireland.
  2. There were many musicians on the boat.
  3. Mona sang at carnivals and shows.
  4. It was cool when Mona arrived in England.
  5. One day, Mona heard about the *Empire Windrush* sailing to England.
  6. Mona loved to play in the sunshine.

- Explain to the children that stories usually follow a specific order of events, so the narrative makes sense as it progresses from start to finish.

- Tell the children that you are going to re-read *We Sang Across the Sea* together and that you want them to pay special attention to what happens when in the book.

- Organise the children into pairs or small groups. Tell them that you have written the main events of the book on the board but not in the correct order. Ask them to work together to decide on the correct order of events and to write them on their whiteboards.

- Call the class together again to ask everyone to share their answers.

> **Differentiation**
> **Extension:** Children retell the story of another book they have read. Start this off by suggesting one which you know they are familiar with and asking them to recall the main sequence of events.

3. Future forecasters

Objective
To read aloud their writing clearly enough to be heard by their peers and the teacher.

What you need
Copies of *We Sang Across the Sea*, photocopiable page 20 'What's the weather today?', a recent weather forecast on the internet.

Cross-curricular links
PSHE, geography

What to do

- Play a recent weather forecast from the internet. Before starting, ask the children to pay attention to the weather words the forecaster uses.

- Afterwards, ask the children what weather words they heard (for example: 'sun', 'rain', 'clouds'). Write these on the board, then add others that were not mentioned, such as 'windy', 'cold', 'hot', 'warm', 'cool', 'storms'.

- Next, show the children how they can put these words into simple weather sentences and write them on the board, for example:

  - Today, it will be sunny/cloudy/windy.
  - There will be storms.
  - It is very cold and windy today.
  - Today's temperature is 20°C.

- Hand out photocopiable page 20, 'What's the weather?'. Ask the children to use the internet to look up today's weather, both in their home town and in Port of Spain, the capital of Trinidad and Tobago, using websites such as BBC Weather or the Met Office.

- Once the children have the day's forecast, ask them to draw the weather symbol(s) for Port of Spain in the box on the photocopiable page and complete the sentences using weather words. Then they do the same for their home town.

- At the end of the lesson, invite volunteers give a weather forecast to the class.

Differentiation
Support: Children can draw the weather symbols based on the descriptions of Trinidad and England in the book.

4. Forties fashion designer

Objective
To give well-structured descriptions, explanations and narratives for different purposes, including for expressing feelings.

What you need
Copies of *We Sang Across the Sea*, photocopiable page 21 'Forties fashion designer', colouring pencils or pens, pictures of 1940s fashions from the internet.

Cross-curricular links
History, art

What to do

- As a class, look at the illustrations in *We Sang Across the Sea* and ask the children to focus on the clothes the people are wearing in the everyday settings (not during Carnival). Remind them that this was in the 1940s. Ask the children if they can tell you:

  - how the clothes are different from what people wear nowadays
  - how they are similar
  - whether they like the clothes or not.

- Differences might include the fact that men wear ties, hats and suits more than they do nowadays, while women are almost always in dresses or skirts (they may mention the style of the dresses and skirts, too, with nipped-in waists and a fuller skirt) and some wear hats. The children might comment on how the people seem to dress more smartly than nowadays. Similarities might include the fact that some women and girls still wear dresses and skirts a lot.

- Show some pictures of the fashions from the 1940s – these are easily found on the internet, and the Imperial War Museum has a short, interesting video on the styles.

- Hand out photocopiable page 21 'Forties fashion designer' and tell the children that you would like them to design an outfit for a man or woman from the 1940s. They can draw it directly onto the human shape on the page. Display pictures of fashion from the 1940s so they can be informed and inspired by them as they work.

- Bring the class together for a fashion show!

5. The Windrush generation

Objective
To participate in discussion about what is read to them, taking turns and listening to what others say.

What you need
Copies of *We Sang Across the Sea*, child-friendly web pages about the Windrush generation.

Cross-curricular links
History, PSHE

What to do
- Read out this text about the Windrush generation:

> After the Second World War, Britain needed lots of help to rebuild the country. But there weren't enough people. The government advertised for workers from countries that were part of the British Empire, and who had served with Britain in the Second World War, to come to Britain to live and work.
>
> On 22 June 1948, around 500 people from the Caribbean arrived in England on board the *Empire Windrush*. They had travelled thousands of miles on a ship across the Atlantic Ocean.
>
> People did not always welcome the new arrivals. Many who came found it hard to find a home and to make friends with British people. Some could not find the work they had been promised because some businesses did not want to hire black people. At school, their children were sometimes bullied because the colour of their skin was different. This unkind behaviour is called racism and discrimination.
>
> Around half a million people came over from the Caribbean to Britain between the years of 1948 and 1971 and they have now been called the Windrush Generation.

- Ask the children their views on how the Windrush generation were treated when they arrived in the UK. Was it fair? Ask them to support their opinions. Ask: *Are things different now?*

- Ask: *Are there any signs of these troubles in We Sang Across the Sea?* (Remind the children of Mona's statement that 'As a Caribbean girl, sometimes I just had to be quite strong'.)

6. Ask the author/illustrator

Objective
To ask relevant questions to extend their understanding and knowledge.

What you need
Copies of *We Sang Across the Sea*, interviews with Benjamin Zephaniah and/or Onyinye Iwu, individual whiteboards.

Cross-curricular link
PSHE

What to do
- Start the lesson by asking the children if they can remember what an author and an illustrator do when a book is being made. You might need to refresh their knowledge.

- Tell the children that they are going to think of questions to ask Benjamin Zephaniah, the author, and Onyinye Iwu, the illustrator, about *We Sang Across the Sea*. Play or show any interviews with either of them on the internet before the activity so the children get an idea of what happens in an interview.

- Give the children five minutes or so to talk in pairs or small groups about the kinds of questions they might like to ask and to write them on their whiteboards.

- Call the class back together and ask for examples of questions. Write them on the board. The questions should include things like:
  - Why did you want to write the book?
  - Is it harder to write a book about a real person than a made-up one?
  - How do you draw your pictures? Do you use a computer?
  - What other books have you written/drawn?
  - Do you think your book is a poem?
  - How do you both work together on a book?

- If there is time, you could role play the interviews, with you or the children taking on the role of Benjamin Zephaniah and/or Onyinye Iwu and trying to answer the questions.

Differentiation
Extension: Children could think of questions they would like to ask other authors or illustrators.

What's the weather today?

- Can you forecast the weather in Trinidad and in your home town? Find out what it is and complete the sentences below, drawing a weather picture for each.

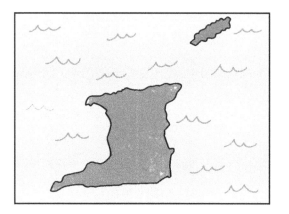

The weather in Trinidad and Tobago today is: _____

_____

The temperature is: _____

_____

I live in: _____

The weather where I live today is: _____

_____

The temperature is: _____

Forties fashion designer

- Design an outfit for a man or woman in the 1940s using the pictures in the book. Draw straight onto the figure below.

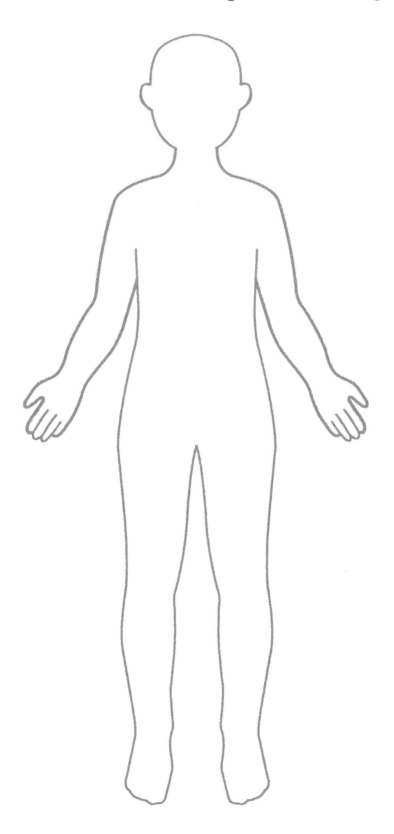

TALK ABOUT IT ▶

1. And your score is...

> ### Objective
> To listen and respond appropriately to adults and peers.
>
> ### What you need
> Copies of *We Sang Across the Sea*, individual whiteboards.
>
> ### Cross-curricular link
> Drama

What to do

- Ask the children why using different tones of voice, or speaking louder or quieter, or putting emotion into the words can be effective when reading a story aloud. (Answers could include because it makes the story more exciting, or scary, or funny, and so on.)

- Tell the children that you are going to read aloud a passage from *We Sang Across the Sea* and they must give you a score out of 5 for how well you read it (5 being the highest) and write it on their whiteboards. They must be honest!

- Read out any extract with the refrain: 'I just want to sing!' The first time you read it, put a lot of expression and intonation into your voice – don't be afraid to exaggerate! When you have finished, ask the children to show you their scores for your performance (they should score you 4 or 5).

- Next, read out the same passage, but do so in the most boring voice you can manage, with no emphasis or expression. Ask the children to score you (you should score no more than 1 or 2).

- Lastly, ask the children which performance they liked best, and why.

> ### Differentiation
> **Extension:** Ask children to have a go themselves and experiment with expression.

2. Leaving home

> ### Objective
> To make inferences on the basis of what is being said and done.
>
> ### What you need
> Copies of *We Sang Across the Sea*.
>
> ### Cross-curricular link
> PSHE

What to do

- Ask the children to look at spread 5, which shows Mona on board the *Empire Windrush*, waving goodbye to her family.

- Tell them to look at the expressions on the passengers' faces. Ask: *What do you think the people are feeling?* (Most of them look very happy, excited and cheerful.) *Why do they feel that way? Might they have other feelings, too? They are about to take a very long journey (three weeks) to a very different country. What else might they feel?* (They might be nervous, worried, scared.)

- Next, read the passage aloud, emphasising Mona's words: 'I was a little nervous, and a bit lonely, and a tear fell from my eye.'

- Ask if Mona looks as if she's feeling like this in the illustration (she is in the red dress, near the middle of the page). Ask: *Why does she look happy when she is feeling like this? Why does Mona feel lonely if she is on a ship full of people? Why is she nervous?*

- Ask if the children can relate any experiences of this to their own lives – when they have had to say goodbye, even if for a short time. Have they ever felt sad but excited? Talk about these experiences together.

3. Goodbye and good luck!

Objective
To participate in discussions, presentations, performances, role play, improvisations and debates.

What you need
Copies of *We Sang Across the Sea*.

Cross-curricular link
PSHE

What to do
- Tell children you are going to re-read the beginning of *We Sang Across the Sea* to them and, this time, you want them to think about Mona's relationship with her family.

- After you have finished reading the first five spreads of the book, ask the children what Mona's family might have felt when she told them that she wanted to leave Trinidad and move to Britain to follow her dream of being a singer. Write up their answers on the board.

- Next, organise the children into pairs and say that one of them is Mona and the other a member of her family, such as her mother, father or one of her sisters.

- Explain that the child playing the family member should ask the child playing Mona questions about why she wants to move to Britain. Write these questions on the board as prompts:
  - Why do you want to go to England?
  - Why can't you stay here?
  - What will you do if you don't like it in England?
  - Can we come to visit you?
  - Will you come back home again?

- The child playing Mona should think carefully about how they could answer these questions based on their reading of the story.

- Encourage pairs to practise asking and answering these questions, thinking about how their character would feel. Then they swap roles.

- Ask volunteers to perform their conversation.

Differentiation
Support: Children discuss how Mona might have felt when she left her family.

4. Sweet dreams

Objective
To consider and evaluate different viewpoints, attending to and building on the contributions of others.

What you need
Copies of *We Sang Across the Sea*, photocopiable page 25 'Sweet dreams', art materials.

Cross-curricular links
PSHE, art and design

What to do
- Ask the children for examples of Mona talking about her dream to become a singer. They should talk about Mona's experiences in Trinidad, her excitement on seeing the poster for the *Empire Windrush*, and what she did after she arrived in England to fulfil her dream. They can also refer to the repeated refrain: 'I just want to sing…'

- Ask the children if there is anything they think Mona should have done differently. Do they agree with what she did to follow her dream? Would they have done the same things? Write the following stems on the board for the children to use when talking about what they think:
  - I believe that…
  - In my opinion…

- Next, organise the children into pairs/small groups to talk about their dreams. Ask questions to prompt discussion. What do they want to do in the future? Is there a job they would really like to do? Where would they like to live? Write some sentence starters on the board to help them:
  - In the future, I would like to be…
  - When I'm older, I would like to live…

- Hand out photocopiable page 25 'Sweet dreams'. Tell the children you want them to draw a picture of their future dream and then complete the sentences underneath in their own words.

- Ask children to share their ideas. Encourage everyone to listen and respond with respect.

Differentiation
Support: Children just draw the pictures.

Extension: Children write more about their dreams.

5. Me and my family

Objective
To link what they read or hear to their own experiences.

What you need
Copies of *We Sang Across the Sea*, individual whiteboards.

Cross-curricular link
PSHE

What to do

- Re-read the first two spreads about how Mona and her family spend time together. Point out what they are doing: walking on the beach, eating fruit from their fruit trees and sitting on the veranda (explain what the word 'veranda' means if necessary). Ask: *Is Mona's family happy? How do they feel?* Encourage the children to look at the characters' facial expressions.

- Next, focus on the description: 'We loved to play in the sunshine; enjoying the cool breeze; dreaming of what to do…' Ask the children if they think Mona and her family have a happy life together. *Do they enjoy spending time with each other? Does it seem like Mona has good memories of her childhood?*

- Next, ask the children to think about how Mona's childhood is similar to and different from their own. For example, it might be similar in the way that Mona and her family go for walks together, but it might be different because the weather isn't as sunny or warm! The children might like to play outside in their garden, but they might not have trees from which to pick their own fruit. Their families might be larger or smaller than Mona's.

- Give the children a few minutes to think about this and encourage them to jot down any ideas on their whiteboards.

- Finally, ask for volunteers to talk about how they spend time with their family when they are not at school or at work. If possible, the children should also compare their family life with Mona's.

6. Moving to music

Objective
To articulate and justify answers, arguments and opinions.

What you need
Access to the internet for calypso and soca songs to play to the children.

Cross-curricular links
Music, PE

What to do

- Explain to the children that they are going to listen to some calypso and soca music, which have their roots in Trinidad and Tobago.

- First, explain that calypso music comes from Trinidad and Tobago, though it is played throughout all of the Caribbean now. It first came from a style of African music that was brought to the Caribbean by enslaved West Africans.

- Play them several clips from calypso songs (you can search for the music on the internet: try the song 'Coconut Calypso', by Perform, which is aimed at children and uses dancing that they could copy). Once they have heard some of the music, ask them what kind of music it is. How does it make them feel? Ask them to justify their opinions.

- Tell them that while calypso is often considered to be happy and relaxed, it is often used to criticise politicians and other people in charge of a country.

- Next, tell them that they are going to listen to some soca music, which is a more modern version of calypso. It began in Port of Spain in Trinidad and mixes the traditional West African music rhythms with those of India. Play them the song 'Follow the Leader' – there is a video by DJ Raphi, which shows them how to dance along to the music. This is great fun but you need a lot of space!

- Finally, ask the children what they think of calypso and soca music. Do they like it? How is it similar to the music they listen to? How is it different? Encourage the children to use their own opinions and experiences when answering.

 **Sweet dreams**

- What do you want to be in the future? Where do you want to live? Draw a picture of yourself doing what you dream of in the future and complete the sentences below.

In the future, I want to be _____

because _____

_____

I will live in _____

GET WRITING ▶

1. Chorus lines

Objective
To say aloud what they are going to write about.

What you need
Copies of *We Sang Across the Sea*, lined paper.

Cross-curricular link
Music

What to do

- Explain that *We Sang Across the Sea* is structured like a song – there are parts that explain the story (which are like verses in music) and a repeated rhyme, which acts as a chorus.

- Can the children identify the part of the story which is its 'chorus'? They should say:

> 'I want to sing.
> I want to sing.
> Singing songs will help me grow,
> I just want the world to know,
> Joy is what I bring,
> So, I just want to sing.'

- Ask the children why it is appropriate that Benjamin Zephaniah wrote the story in this way (because Mona Baptiste was a singer).

- Next, hand out the lined paper and tell the children that you would like them to try writing a different chorus for the story. It doesn't have to be as long as the one in the book, but it should say something about Mona Baptiste and her life. Brainstorm what these ideas could be and write suggestions on the board before asking the children to write them down on their paper.

Differentiation
Support: Children could write one or two lines instead of an entire chorus.

2. Proper punctuation

Objective
To begin to punctuate sentences using a capital letter and a full stop, question mark or exclamation mark.

What you need
Individual whiteboards.

What to do

- Tell the children that you are going to look at how to write proper sentences.

- Ask if anyone knows how to start a sentence (you always use a capital letter).

- Next, ask the children for the three different punctuation marks they can use to end a sentence. Write a full stop, an exclamation mark and a question mark on the board. Ask: When would you use each one?

  - A full stop is for normal sentences.
  - A question mark is for asking questions. These often begin with words such as: who, what, when, where, why, how and do.
  - An exclamation mark is used at the end of sentences that show strong emotion, such as surprise, excitement, happiness, anger and fear.

- Next, write the following sentences on the board:
  1. mona has four sisters
  2. why does Mona want to be a singer in England
  3. there's Mona, the famous singer – look
  4. where is Trinidad
  5. mona's dreams came true

- Ask the children to write these sentences on their whiteboards, using capitals and correct punctuation. When they have finished, go through the answers.

Differentiation
Extension: Children write their own sentences about *We Sang Across the Sea*, with correct punctuation and capitals.

3. A postcard home

Objective
To sequence sentences to form short narratives.

What you need
Copies of *We Sang Across the Sea*, pieces of blank paper/paper with a postcard template.

Cross-curricular link
PSHE

What to do

- Tell the children that you would like them to pretend they are Mona Baptiste. They are going to write a postcard home as if they were Mona writing to her family after arriving in England.

- To refresh their memories of events, you could re-read the story to the children, up to and including spread 7, where Mona talks about arriving in England and starting her singing career in clubs and on radio and television. Children should refer to their copies as needed.

- Hand out either blank pieces of paper or search for postcard templates online that you can print out and give to the children. You could explain that this used to be one of the main ways that people communicated when they travelled, before mobile phones and the internet existed.

- Ask the children to pretend they are Mona writing to her family about her experiences since leaving Trinidad. They won't know everything of course, so it's fine for them to use their imagination to fill in the gaps. They could write about:
  - how they felt on board the ship as it left home (waving goodbye, tears, and so on)
  - life on board the ship during the three weeks it took to travel from Trinidad to England (refer to the musicians and bands)
  - what it was like arriving in England (cooler weather – but then the summer soon arrived)
  - how Mona started trying to find work.
- When they have finished, children could read out their postcards.

Differentiation
Support: Children write just a couple of sentences about how they were feeling as the ship left. Direct them to spread 5 in the book.

4. The story of Mona Baptiste

Objective
To write narratives about personal experiences and those of others.

What you need
Copies of *We Sang Across the Sea*, photocopiable page 29 'The Story of Mona Baptise', access to the internet.

Cross-curricular link
History

What to do

- Ask the children if they know what a biography is. Explain, or remind them, that a biography is a story about someone's life that has been written by someone else. In *We Sang Across the Sea* Benjamin Zephaniah is the person writing the biography about Mona Baptiste in a poem or song form.

- Tell the children to write a biography about Mona Baptiste, using the information included in *We Sang Across the Sea* – both in the main part of the book and in the biography at the back. They can also look up information on the internet.

- Hand out photocopiable page 29 'The Story of Mona Baptiste'. Help the children complete the first section together, explaining any new words such as 'birth' and 'occupation', as follows:
  - Date of birth: 1928
  - Place of birth: Port of Spain, Trinidad
  - Occupation: Singer and actress
- Tell the children to write anything they find interesting about Mona in the section 'What I know about Mona'. Advise them to think about important parts of her life, such as leaving home, travelling by ship, and trying to become a well-known singer. They could mention her bravery and her fears, too.

- Invite volunteers to share their biographies with the rest of the class. This would make a nice classroom display, too, with pictures of Mona, the *Empire Windrush* and Trinidad.

Differentiation
Support: Children should write about just one aspect of Mona's life.

5. Carnival!

Objective
To discuss what they have written with the teacher or other pupils.

What you need
Copies of *We Sang Across the Sea*, photocopiable page 30 'Carnival!'.

Cross-curricular link
Geography

What to do

- Tell the children they are going to find out about Carnival in Trinidad.

- Look at spread 3 in the book. Read the text and then ask the children to tell you what they notice about the way people are dressed and what they are doing. They should talk about the vibrant colours and the creative costumes, as well as the use of musical instruments.

- Next, hand out photocopiable page 30 'Carnival!' and read through it with the children, explaining any words they may find difficult. You might like to display photographs or videos from the internet of different aspects of Carnival activities, such as the parades, costumes, music and limbo dancing so they can get a better idea of what Carnival involves. You could also explain that it is celebrated just before Lent begins (Shrove Tuesday is the final day of Carnival) and that other countries in the world also celebrate Carnival, such as Spain and Italy, although perhaps in different ways.

- Once you have talked through the information together, tell the children that you would like them to think about what they have learned and to complete the sentences on the photocopiable page. They should explain why they would like to go to Carnival (or not, if that's the case!) and what they would most like to do.

- At the end of the lesson, ask for volunteers to share their thoughts with the rest of the class.

Differentiation
Support: Children draw a picture of one of Carnival's activities.

6. Book review

Objective
To encapsulate what they want to say, sentence by sentence.

What you need
Copies of *We Sang Across the Sea*, lined paper or book review template, online book reviews.

What to do

- Begin by asking the children if they know what a book review is. Once you have taken their suggestions, consolidate by explaining that a good book review:
  - summarises what the book is about, without giving away the ending
  - says something about the main character(s)
  - tells you what is good and not so good about the book
  - gives an honest opinion.

- Show the children some examples by looking up 'Children's book reviews' on the internet. (There are sites where children have written reviews of books – have these ready in advance.)

- Read out the reviews and ask the children why the reviews are helpful, or not. Have they read any of the books? Do they agree with the reviews?

- Next, hand out the blank paper or book review template and tell the children that you would like them to write a book review about *We Sang Across the Sea*, using everything they can remember about the story. They should include:
  - title of book
  - name of author and illustrator
  - what the book is about
  - why they liked the book (or not)
  - whether they recommend the book.

- They could also draw a picture of a scene in the book that they particularly enjoyed.

Differentiation
Support: Children write about their favourite part of the book.

Extension: Provide internet access for children to search for more children's book reviews.

The story of Mona Baptiste

- Use the prompts below to write a biography of Mona Baptiste.

Date of birth:

_____

Place of birth:

_____

_____

Occupation:

_____

What I know about Mona Baptiste:

_____

_____

_____

_____

_____

_____

_____

_____

Carnival!

- Read the text below about Carnival in Trinidad. Write why you would like to go and what you would like to do the most.

There is a saying in Trinidad: "Trinidadians never stop thinking about Carnival." This might be why Trinidad has one of the best Carnivals in the world!

Carnival is celebrated every year in February or March. There are huge parades and people dress up in colourful costumes called 'mas'. They dance in the streets to either calypso or soca music.

There is also limbo dancing, a very difficult dance which started in Trinidad. People must bend backwards to go underneath a stick without touching it with their body or knocking it off. The stick gets lower and lower. The winner is the person who can go the lowest without making it fall off or touching it.

I would like to go to Carnival because:

_____

_____

The thing I would like to do most is:

_____

_____

ASSESSMENT ▶

---

1. What can you remember?

> **Objective**
> To explain clearly their understanding of what is read to them.
>
> **What you need**
> Copies of *We Sang Across the Sea*, individual whiteboards.

What to do

- Tell the children you are going to give them a fun quiz about what they can remember about reading *We Sang Across the Sea*. You can either read the book with them one more time before doing this quiz, or let them have a look through a copy themselves or with a partner.

- Read out and/or write on the board the following questions. The children should write their answers on their whiteboards without talking to their classmates or friends.
  1. Which island is Mona from?
  2. How many sisters did Mona have?
  3. How did Mona travel to England?
  4. How did Mona feel when she left her family?
  5. What was the weather like when she arrived in England?
  6. Where could people hear Mona sing?
  7. How did Mona's family feel about her?

- Read each of the questions a couple of times to give the children a chance to understand what they mean and to think of their answers. Once they are finished, go through the answers with the whole class, asking children to give their answers. Tell the children not to worry if they misspell something. (Answers: 1. Trinidad; 2. four; 3. boat (*Empire Windrush*); 4. nervous/sad/worried/scared; 5. cool/cold; 6. television/clubs/radio; 7. proud)

2. Creative writing

> **Objective**
> To learn how to use expanded noun phrases to describe and specify.
>
> **What you need**
> Copies of *We Sang Across the Sea*, individual whiteboards.

What to do

- Ask the children if they know or can remember what an expanded noun phrase is (a noun with one or more adjectives describing it). Write some examples on the board, progressing from the simple phrases to more detailed ones, for example:
  - a black cat
  - a fat, black cat
  - a scary, fat, black cat.

- Next, write the following expanded noun phrases from *We Sang Across the Sea* on the board:
  - 'the cool breeze'
  - 'a great delight'
  - 'the great big ship'
  - 'a singing sensation'.

- Ask if the children can think of any ways to change these into something else (for example, 'an icy breeze'; 'the enormous ship').

- Tell the children that there aren't many expanded noun phrases in the book. Ask them to help you to make the nouns more interesting by expanding the ones below:
  1. the stage
  2. the sea
  3. the summer
  4. a tear
  5. the islands
  6. the animals
  7. the moon
  8. a singer

- Encourage the children to be creative. Model some possibilities to get them started, for example: 'the wooden stage'; 'the sparkling, emerald sea'. Children can work in pairs or small groups, using their whiteboards before sharing ideas as a class.

3. This and that

Objective

To develop their understanding of the concepts set out in English Appendix 2 by joining words and joining clauses using 'and'.

What you need

Copies of *We Sang Across the Sea*, lined paper.

What to do

- Tell the children that you are all going to look at how to use the joining word 'and' in sentences. Explain that a joining word is also known as a 'conjunction'.

- Next, tell the children that the word 'and' can be used in different ways as a joining word: either to add more information to a simple sentence ('At school we learn about words <u>and</u> numbers.') or to join two different phrases or short sentences together ('In the morning I eat breakfast <u>and</u> then I go to school.').

- Explain that by joining two shorter sentences to make one longer one, they can make their writing more interesting.

- Hand out sheets of lined paper and then write the following sentences on the board in two columns.

1. The sun shines a lot in Trinidad.	Sometimes it rains.
2. Mona sang to people.	She also sang to animals.
3. Mona was a little bit nervous.	She was lonely, too.
4. There were many musicians on the boat.	They played in many bands.
5. Mona sang in clubs.	She was also on the radio.

- Tell the children that they are going to join the sentences on the left with the ones on the right using the joining word 'and' to make one complete sentence, for example: 'The sun shines a lot in Trinidad and sometimes it rains.' Ask them to do this for each pair.

- When they have finished, check their work.

Differentiation

Extension: Children make up their own sentences about Mona Baptiste or the book in general.

4. The moral of the story is…

Objective

To use spoken language to develop understanding through speculating, hypothesising, imagining and exploring ideas.

What you need

Copies of *We Sang Across the Sea*.

What to do

- Begin the lesson by asking the children if they know what a 'moral' is in a story. (It is the lesson the reader should learn because of what has happened in the story.)

- Ask the children why stories often have morals in them. (to help explain an important point to the reader so they understand the main message of the book)

- Ask the children if they can give you any examples of books or stories they have read or heard where the main character or characters have learned a lesson at the end. Traditional tales often have these, for example, 'The Gingerbread Man'. The children should be familiar with this tale but, if not, tell them the story and then ask what the moral is. (Don't trust strangers./Be careful who you trust.) Write any examples and the morals on the board.

- Explain that bad things don't necessarily have to happen to the main characters in stories with morals or lessons. Their function could be to encourage readers to achieve their potential, to be brave or creative, for example. Or they could show readers how to overcome a difficulty they may have, such as making friends or keeping their temper.

- Once you have explored these ideas, ask: *What have we learned by reading this book*? Children may offer different answers here, but they should generally be: believe in yourself, keep trying to achieve what you want, believe anything is possible, have faith in your dreams, don't let others put you down.